W9-CPF-160

A Tall, Tall Giant

Story by Janie Spaht Gill, Ph.D.
Illustrations by Elizabeth Lambson

DOMINIE PRESS
Pearson Learning Group

A tall, tall giant

went through
a tall, tall gate,

across a tall, tall
porch,

through a tall, tall door,

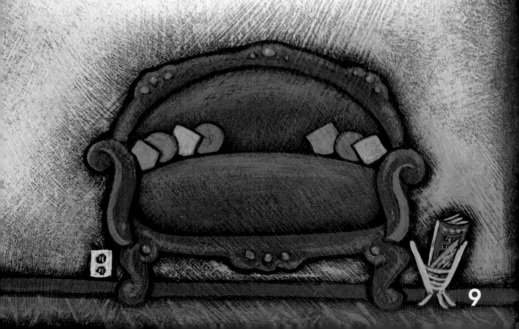

into a tall, tall house,

down a tall, tall hall,

up some tall, tall steps,

15

into a tall, tall attic,

where a teeny, tiny mouse,
in a teeny hole said,
"Squeak! Squeak! Squeak!"